3.

This book is to be returned o
the last date

Chocolate

Claire Llewellyn

W
FRANKLIN WATTS
LONDON•SYDNEY

First published in 2004
by Franklin Watts
96 Leonard Street
London EC2A 4XD

Franklin Watts Australia
45-51 Huntley Street
Alexandria NSW 2015

Series advisor: Gill Matthews, non-fiction literacy consultant and Inset trainer
Editor: Caryn Jenner
Series design: Peter Scoulding
Designer: James Marks
Photography: Ray Moller unless otherwise credited
Acknowledgements: Stephen Coyne/Ecoscene: 6. Elleringmann/Laif/AURORA: 13. Ron Giling/Still
Pictures: 12. Martin Gilmour/Masterfoods: 11. Masterfoods: 1, 10, 16, 17, 18, 22bl. Christine
Osborne/Ecoscene: 7, 22cr. Jorgen Schytte/Still Pictures: 8-9.
Thanks to our models: Khailam Palmer Mutlu, Scarlett Carney, Casey Liu.

A CIP catalogue record for this book is available from the British Library

ISBN: 0 7496 5417 1

Printed in Malaysia

Contents

Mmmm! Chocolate! 4

Chocolate is made from beans 6

The cocoa pods 8

Drying the beans 10

At the chocolate factory 12

Cocoa powder 14

Making chocolate 16

The chocolate cools 18

Chocolate is a treat 20

I know that… 22

Index 24

About this book 24

Mmmm! Chocolate!

Many people eat chocolate. Some people like chocolate so much that it is their favourite food.

We eat chocolate in many different ways.

What is your favourite way of eating chocolate?

5

Chocolate is made from beans

Chocolate is made from cocoa beans. The beans grow in pods on the cacao tree.

▶ *Cocoa pods grow on the trunks of cacao trees.*

Each cocoa pod is filled with sticky, white beans.

There are about 40 cocoa beans in every pod.

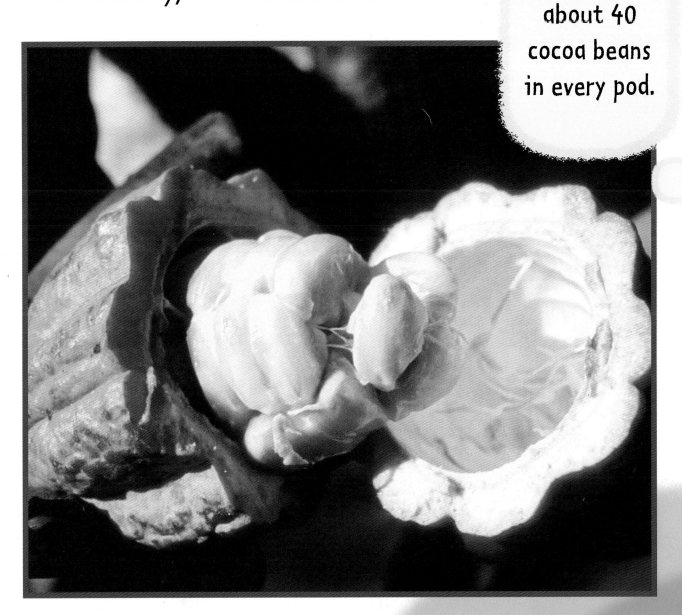

The cocoa pods

Cocoa pods are small at first. After six months, they are big and ripe.

▶ *The ripe cocoa pods are cut off the trees.*

Cacao trees grow best in the shady parts of hot, wet rainforests.

Drying the beans

The cocoa beans are taken out of the pods and left to dry in the sun.

How are these dried beans different from the beans in the pod on page 7?

10

▲ Workers turn the beans so they
dry all over. Workers wear hats
as shade from the hot sun.

At the chocolate factory

The dried cocoa beans are sent to the chocolate factory.

Sacks of cocoa beans are sent to factories.

The beans are washed and roasted. Then they are mashed into a paste called cocoa mass.

Cocoa mass tastes very bitter.

▲ *This machine mashes the cocoa beans.*

Cocoa powder

Some cocoa mass is dried to make cocoa powder.

▼ *If we add cocoa powder to a cake...*

...the cake will have a chocolate taste.

What is the difference between chocolate drinking powder and cocoa powder? Taste a little of both and see.

Making chocolate

Some cocoa mass is mixed with milk and sugar to make chocolate.

▶ *When it is first made, chocolate is runny.*

Try some dark chocolate, white chocolate and milk chocolate. Can you taste the difference?

▲ *The runny chocolate is poured over biscuits and cakes or made into chocolate bars.*

The chocolate cools

Runny chocolate goes hard as it cools.

▷ *When these chocolate bars are cool, they will be wrapped up for sale.*

▲ *Chocolate can be made into different shapes.*

What happens to chocolate when you hold it in your hand for too long? It melts!

Chocolate is a treat

Chocolate is a special treat, but too much chocolate is not good for us.

▶ *A few squares of a chocolate bar is a treat...*

▲ ...*so is a chocolate from a box.*

Ask an adult to help you make chocolate-covered cornflake treats. Stir some cornflakes into a bowl of melted chocolate. Spoon the mixture into paper cases and cool.

◀ *We should eat lots of different foods. Then a little chocolate is good as a treat.*

I know that...

1 Many people eat chocolate.

2 Chocolate is made from cocoa beans.

3 Cocoa beans grow inside pods on cacao trees.

4 The beans are taken out of the pods and dried.

5 The beans are washed, roasted and mashed into a paste.

6 Some of the paste is dried to make cocoa powder.

7 Milk and sugar are added to the paste to make chocolate.

8 Chocolate goes hard when it cools, and melts when it gets warm.

9 Too much chocolate is not good for us.

Index

biscuits 17

cacao tree 6, 8, 9, 22

cake 14, 15, 17

chocolate

  bars 17, 18, 20

  factory 12

cocoa

  bean 6, 7, 10, 11,
    12, 13, 22, 23

  mass 13, 14, 16

  pod 6, 7, 8, 10, 22

  powder 14, 15, 23

drinking powder 15

melts 19, 23

milk 16, 17, 23

rainforest 9

sugar 16, 23

About this book

I Know That! is designed to introduce children to the process of gathering information and using reference books, one of the key skills needed to begin more formal learning at school. For this reason, each book's structure reflects the information books children will use later in their learning career – with key information in the main text and additional facts and ideas in the captions. The panels give an opportunity for further activities, ideas or discussions. The contents page and index are helpful reference guides.

The language is carefully chosen to be accessible to children just beginning to read. Illustrations support the text but also give information in their own right; active consideration and discussion of images is another key referencing skill. The main aim of the series is to build confidence – showing children how much they already know and giving them the ability to gather new information for themselves. With this in mind, the *I know that...* section at the end of the book is a simple way for children to revisit what they already know as well as what they have learnt from reading the book.